Accelerated Learning Techniques For Beginners:

Effective Tips to Improve Your Memory and Reading Comprehension , Learn More and Faster, Enhance Intellect

By

Dale Blake

Table of Contents

Introduction 5

Chapter 1. The truth About Learning 6

Chapter 2. How to Improve Your Pace in Learning 8

Chapter 3. How to Boost Memory and Comprehension 16

Final Words 29

Thank You Page 30

Accelerated Learning Techniques For Beginners: Effective Tips to Improve Your Memory and Reading Comprehension, Learn More and Faster, Enhance Intellect

By Dale Blake

© Copyright 2014 Dale Blake

Reproduction or translation of any part of this work beyond that permitted by section 107 or 108 of the 1976 United States Copyright Act without permission of the copyright owner is unlawful. Requests for permission or further information should be addressed to the author.

This publication is designed to provide accurate and authoritative information in regard to the subject matter covered. This work is sold with the understanding that the publisher is not engaged in rendering legal, accounting, or other professional services. If legal advice or other expert assistance is required, the services of a competent professional person should be sought.

First Published, 2014

Printed in the United States of America

Introduction

In school, there are kids who are so quick to pick up a mathematical formula, to memorize a poem, to get the principles behind a mechanism, to distinguish differences between and among similar words, to read such lengthy books and do amazing reports on them. There are kids, too, who would struggle to write down what the teacher has written before the notes disappear from the board, spend all night trying to finish half a chapter of a novel, or seek professional help to learn the basics of fractions.

At work it could be so difficult to keep up with deadlines on reports, articles, reviews and minutes. Everything could seem too fast that you sometimes blame your boss for being too demanding, when the truth is you need some stretching in certain skills, which could make you a better employee, a more excellent student, a more productive person.

Chapter 1. The truth About Learning

Before getting to some practical ways to becoming a better version of yourself in terms of learning, realize and accept first, that indeed, life is not fair. Doing so will increase your chances of avoiding comparison of yourself with others, and preventing yourself from being distracted by others' seemingly more developed cognition, making you miss the chance of realizing that your innate unique strengths will bring you to the attainment of your goals.

People do not have the same brain waves. This partly explains why there are factions in society, why there are groups in Facebook, why there are sections in grade school, why there are choices of programs to enroll in college, and why organizations have departments. People are not the same, hence not all people are brainiacs. Some are more adept with certain skills, while others can only excel in other forms of talent. In fact, more and more experts try to prove, debunk, and then prove again certain learning theories that state that there are various intelligences.

However, what is constant among human beings is the uncontrollable need to learn.

In dealing with a need, one has to satisfy it, much more importantly than how a want, the lower form of it, must be gratified. Some people say than learning is natural and not forced, while others argue that in order to learn, one must invest deliberately, exerting efforts. The more you invest, the more you learn, they say. If learning is effortless, therefore, why do some people find it so hard to grasp certain information? Why is there a need to spend so much energy on trying to memorize and comprehend?

Chapter 2. How to Improve Your Pace in Learning

While the need to learn is not a choice, the drive to improve on learning is enormously optional. To be excellent on something is significantly influenced by the will to do so, and in turn, becoming better in terms of memory and comprehension entails effort. But for efforts to become more of a pleasure, it lessens the burden by half if you approach the 'struggle' with the right disposition. Here are some things that will help you unburden yourself of the seemingly stringent nature of learning, especially if you are a student.

Have a positive attitude

The things you intend to learn are not always as interesting as those you already know. There are times when you cannot help but display a negative attitude about learning. In cases like this, a realization that excuses are fabricated in an attempt to outwit the issue at hand, is necessary, and what strengthens such lies is the pride that hides underneath them.

Therefore, it is worth noting that pride is what keeps you from becoming a better learner.

The primary solution: be humble. It has been said that in order to learn, one must have the humility to unlearn. Thinking that you know enough will make you miss on the many exciting things to still discover. Thinking that you need not improve, even indirectly, deprives you of the experience to upgrade yourself. To unlearn means to acknowledge and recognize that some of what you know may need some updates, just as some software on your mobile gadget becomes obsolete. The ability to acknowledge and recognize such is only possible when you get rid of that filthy pride.

Other than humility, positivity is also important. Sometimes you just feel hopeless and helpless, as you get discouraged with the difficulties your tasks seem to bring you. In order for you to see the brighter side of having to accomplish some paperwork, go back to your ultimate goal of studying (or of working, for that matter). But first, what is your goal – your *ultimate* goal?

Establish your ultimate goal

Your decision of going to school to learn may have been influenced by several factors. You may have probably been given a scholarship, which you think not worth the snub. You may have been forced by your current job to get a degree so you may keep it. You may also have been driven by peer pressure, as most, if not all of your friends are doing the same thing. These apparently superficial factors may be secondary, as they are external by nature, but indeed, they have provoked you to get in.

However, there is still this one reason you decided to do what you have done. Despite external encouragement, on the positive side, or pressure, on the other, there is still one deeper reason you decided to study – more profound than getting that job, or pleasing your benefactor, or fitting in your social circle. No matter what you choose to believe your reasons are, you could have backed out had you been truly disinterested. Therefore, you decided because part of you wanted to. You took what it takes to be in there because you want to be a better person.

So in case you feel like you are losing reasons to solve that math problem, or read that book so thick, or memorize that boring poem, remember that nobody is going to push you best but yourself. Nothing is going to make you an improved learner better than your very own goals.

Concentrate

Before you get to rid yourself of what keeps you from learning better, you have to know what tends to be stronger than your drive to focus on finish reading at selection at a given time, or on memorizing what you are required to. Be aware of your distractions, and find ways to eliminate them.

Concentration is key to successful learning – be it reading, listening, or the interactive approach. Before you get to eliminate distractions, your awareness should lead you to writing them down, just like a wish list, and tick each item off once you have learned to get rid of them. In this way, you will also be able to have a sense of accomplishment, and may be motivated further to keep being self-aware, and to keep improving.

So, what are some of your distractions? It is noise? Use your headphones. Is the music not helping? Go find a more conducive place to study. Do you lack the right vocabulary? Grab a dictionary. Do you learn better in a group? Make good friends! Are you simply lacking of motivation? Go back to items 1 and 2. Are you too stressed with certain emotions? Read on.

Overcome emotional stress

While some say that stress is not always bad, even its so-called good kind causes you distraction. It drains your energy so badly that your concentrating powers may seem to have never existed. In order to make use of your energy more wisely, do not allow this **state of mental tension and worry caused by anything ruin your drive. Not only does emotional stress drain you emotionally, it also manifests in your physique.**

In order to be able to manage your stress – whether pending or existent, you should first identify its source.

Ask yourself what the root cause of what makes you worry is. Second, know how your present state can address this source by determining your strengths and making them work against these stressors. Keep this formula in mind, and be on your toes for whatever impending anxiety may be approaching.

Make learning enjoyable

As you overcome emotional stress, counter it further by doing what makes you happy. Give yourself some slack, and treat yourself with your favorite ice cream. Buy yourself the wardrobe you have been checking out for months. Pamper yourself with the body spa you deserve. Make sure to do what it takes to be a stress-free learner. By associating things that you enjoy with learning, the discovery process becomes more of a pleasurable experience. It is like making learning the means to an end, which is rewarding yourself.

In addition to associating the good and happy things with your cognitive achievements, you can further make learning a delightful experience by turning learning itself into the very end of all your efforts. If you get to the point of considering your discoveries, your improvements, or your mastery of certain skills the very reward (more than ice cream or body massage) you get from all your hardwork (the means), then you have reached a milestone in your commitment to learning.

Once you have found yourself with a better disposition to learn more, you become more receptive to the following ways on improving not only learning speed, but more importantly, quality. Memory and comprehension are two distinct learning skills that are essential to develop at all ages. Although they are sometimes discussed together, as in reading and in listening, they are two entirely different things, whose strategies for improvement may be similar. For example, after reading a book, one may be able to remember details and even exact lines, but may have difficulty in retelling the story. Another may be a natural in presenting the contents all over, but hardly memorizes a line. Memorization and comprehension are two different things. But both memorization and comprehension in reading requires reading, and those in listening require listening. Added to reading and listening is the classic need to concentrate. This is how it goes generally. For other specific ways though, please read on.

Chapter 3. How to Boost Memory and Comprehension

Be healthy

They key to any successful task is to make your body able to function at its best. While your brain indeed controls your body, and studying uses a great deal of your head, your brain is still part of your body, and you must nourish it, give it the right balance in rest and activity.

Eat right

What you ingest (and refuse to take it), they say defines you. This is one thing to know. More specifically, consider that what you digest is a vital factor in improving your memory, or making it deteriorate. When you were told as a child to eat a balance diet, to be strong, there was truth to that. Doing so also holds true to making you smarter.

A perspective in medicine considers your digestive system as the 'second brain', as the normal flora of bacteria in your gut is said to send signal to your brain through the vagal nerve, one of the cranial nerves that somehow connects the brain to your gut. Some of the neurons present in both your brain and your digestive tract are those that develop neurotransmitters like serotonin, which is connected with mood. This goes to say that gut health affects your brain health, and so keeping your digestive system healthy makes you keep your brain healthy too.

If you do not like fresh vegetables, try them. Love them. Eat them. They, along with healthy fats and food that are not rich in simple glucose and grains, are said to boost the power of your body's powerhouse. Foods that contain antioxidants and other compounds make your brain healthier, and may even spur the production of fresh, new brain cells. What a boost to your memory that is.

There are also brain supplements that aide in boosting your memory capacity. Vitamin D intake, for instance, helps increase healthy growth of nerve in your brain, and improves its abilities to plan, process information, and form new memories. Increasing levels of vitamin D has also been proven to help keep older adults become more mentally fit. Be sure to expose yourself to sunlight though so that your body stores of vitamin D, as well as your supplemental intake, gets absorbed in your blood stream, thereby increasing you brain function.

Also, since as mentioned above, good bacteria are what send signals to the brain via the vagus nerve, then an intake of probiotics may also help in keeping your mind healthy. Probiotics have been proven to have a link in improving your brain's health, in its contribution to your gut's healthy condition. These can be sourced out from fermented food, like kimchi, a Korean side dish, miso, or fermented tofu which is popular in Japan, and yogurt.

Sleep well

Various studies have proven to enhance your memories, simply because it makes you healthy. Rest is necessary, as it is inevitable. It may be considered a limitation, but a better perspective will allow you to view it as an opportunity to allow your physical body to become more functional, your brain to be more healthy, hence more receptive to information.

Sleep, along with proper nutrition, is so basic a human need, that any activity can be dependent on its adequacy. Even babies' brainpower can be given significant boost by naps – what they do most of the time, aside from cooing and breastfeeding. In a study, it was found that, infants who slept in between learning and testing sessions had a better ability to recognize patterns in new information, which signals an important change in memory that plays an essential role in cognitive development. Quite possible that is also true for adults, simply because even among adults, a mid-day nap can help to significantly boost and restore brainpower. A lot of adults even refer to a quick nap as a 'power nap', and which power must they be referring to? Definitely, it is your brain's.

Giving your brain enough rest allows you to concentrate at longer periods, thereby encourages memorization better. It gives you more uninterrupted time to study, and a more solid capacity to absorb what you study by reading, listening, or discussing with a group.

Exercise

Providing a great deal of spur to the body for better performance, exercise also gives the brain significant stimulation in its every endeavor. It does so by motivating the brain to function at its fullest by working on the multiplication of neurons, thereby keeping their networks strong and undamaged.
So if you find yourself staring at a book for more than necessary, wasting too much of your time in the library trying to force information in your head, probably it's time you hit the gym or the running track, as your eyes may be awake, but you are actually brain-asleep. Get your neurons going by getting some stimulation from that 30-minute jog.

Strategize

In any endeavor, your strategies define your game. While is planning your move is something that needs no spelling out, as it may be too basic to over-discuss, remember than other than your goals, your interventions are crucial. If your goal is to be able to memorize more in a shorter span, know which techniques you can employ. Check out the following, and see which ones you can do.

Take one task at a time

You have heard it time and again that concentration is key. But what if you have problems concentrating? If you have already identified the things that distract you from the earlier mention, and still find problems concentrating, maybe there's one more thing you were not able to include in your list.

When reading a material, do you do this one selection at a time? Do you start from the very beginning, or do you browse each page for a more interesting part? Is your television on? When reading from the computer, how many windows are active?

The tendency of having so many tasks to do is trying to do them altogether. While some may find themselves comfortable doing such, you may doubt that they accomplish more doing so, that focusing on one task at a time. Multitasking robs you of a good momentum that leads to a better absorption of the points you need to study. It may make you appear busy, successful and smart, but I would not make you less of a person if you choose to work on one thing, finish it, and move on to another. This strategy will save you more time, and will give you better quality of learning.

Also, multitasking has been proven to give you memory alright, but more of the short-term one. In fact, it oftentimes encourages forgetfulness – the exact opposite of what you would like to develop. Mindfulness can only be achieved best when you concentrate, and stop multitasking.

Stay in a more conducive environment

Among other distractions already mentioned is the very place where your studying seems to be unsuccessful. How conducive is your room for studying? Is your source of light adequate? If not, this may strain your eyes, wasting much of your energy. Is your place well-ventilated? You may not be breathing the right amount of gases, rendering you light-headed.

Do you have noisy housemates, or classmates around? Maybe you need to stay elsewhere.

Studying may be comparable to sleeping and eating, when considering the environment in which you do it. It takes an excellent bed to make your sleeping experience comfortable, and it takes an appealing dining room to make you enjoy your time to consume your meals. In studying, you would surely want meet your goals, just as you need to sleep well and eat right. Choose the venue that best suits your reading needs, and discover how much impact it may offer.

Do not just read

When talking about memory, reading is one of the things that may instantly cross your mind. You usually read what you need to remember. When you need to master the lyrics of a song you have in your playlist, you not only listen to it; you sometimes also have to write the words, so that you can sing along while reading. When preparing for a report in class, you jot down notes on a cue card, and try to keep them in mind (although you sometime glance on them). Even theater artists need to read a script prior to their memory of it.

So reading is essential. In fact, you take down notes during a lecture so that you would have a copy of what you need to keep in mind. However, just reading these may need some booster, too. What can be a modified type of studying by reading, is reading out loud. It is one thing that you listened to your lecturer, and it is another thing to have written them down and read your notes. What is even better is listening to it over and over, by reading them to yourself aloud several times. Some even record themselves while reading, so that they can play the recording even when they are in bed, where lights are out, and eyes are shut.

Find study buddies

Another strategy that may come after this is having a study group comprised of people with the same goal. This may not only serve as an enhancement on your study environment, but also as an audience when you need to speak out loud the ideas that you would like to keep remembering. Keeping the group exclusive to those who share the same objectives in learning allows you a support system that would most likely not be tired of listening to each other, as their interest of the same things will keep them even excited to meet up.

Together, you can do several activities that may help you more in increasing your memory and comprehension.

Play brain games

Brain games have been studied and proven to be effective in reducing brain deterioration, and thereby, in improving brain function, specifically critical thinking, memorization, analysis, comprehension, and other higher order thinking skills. There is a number or brain games that are available (but are not limited to) online and offline, and on board. It may sound childish at first, but there are age-appropriate brain games that may help you stimulate your brain neurons.
In order to avoid defeating the purpose of playing brain games, invest a minimum of 20 minutes a day, with at most seven minutes on specific tasks.

Explore other skills

Psychology proposes a comprehensive way of appreciating an individual's capacities, measuring one's intelligence not only through one's academic performance, but also of other facts through its so-called multiple intelligences.

Being adept in other skills especially the higher order thinking skills (HOTS) helps your memory and comprehension skills improve in different ways. First, in employing HOTS, your analytic skills are activated, which further contributes to not only memorizing concepts, but most especially of understanding them, and their implications. Second, one important HOTS is critical thinking. In the process of enhancing memory and comprehension, you not only grasp concepts, but also learn how to utilize them in other more practical situations when appropriate and necessary. Last, your creative skills are intertwined with an effective memory and comprehension strategy. The arcane process of teaching techniques in memorizing and comprehending needs innovation through the use of creativity, which is equally significant with other HOTS.

One appreciates a technique if it is creatively utilized. There are various ways in which skills are further developed through other skills. This is basically because the brain is actively functioning, thus is more capable of absorbing information to a better and more improved ability to memorize and comprehend. This also paves the way to an improved and holistic self.

Exploring other skills alone may be effective too, but keeping yourself company in doing would lead you to better results. Knowing a wider array of skills to learn from your study buddies can give you more options to choose from. Not only will the group be helpful with such knowledge, but more ultimately, being your support system, your group can encourage you towards this holism you may be able to achieve.

Use mnemonics

Mnemonic devices, or mnemonic aids come from a Greek word meaning 'to bring to mind'. Simply, these devices are tools for your memory to help you more quickly remember words or information, and to organize concepts into a format that is much easier to understand.

Utilizing mnemonics enhances memory and is useful in learning seemingly overwhelming amounts of information that apparently lack pattern, making them look unrelated. These aids are more effective for memorization rather than comprehension. Some mnemonic examples include rhymes, acronyms, catch phrases, association by image, and peg words.

Memorizing concepts by playing with them intelligently but practically can be done alone, or with your study group. You may be surprised how your ideas may contribute significantly to what your study buddies already know, and vice-versa. Besides, turning studying into a more fun-filled experience increases your chances to learn effortlessly.

Final Words

Of course, the more comprehensive list of tips to make your learning skills better gets longer and longer over time, but one ultimate technique that tops it all is what you might hear just all the time, since you were trying to walk, talk, ride a bike, swim, sing, read, write, invent something, play an instrument, and advance on a talent. It has been long believed that repetition leads to mastery, and that no repetition can ever occur without even starting. So in case you have not yet started, now is your chance to do that jumpstart. As you do so, keep in mind that the best way to keep improving is to practice, and to never stop doing it.

Indeed there will never be perfect learning, as there does not seem to be an end in learning. But if you decide and act to aim for perfection in your efforts to practice everything listed above, that only leads you to no chance of stopping. Learning is truly an unending process, and hopefully, you get to find the will to make your commitment to improve learning as eternal as learning itself.

Thank You Page

I want to personally thank you for reading my book. I hope you found information in this book useful and I would be very grateful if you could leave your honest review about this book. I certainly want to thank you in advance for doing this.

www.ingramcontent.com/pod-product-compliance
Lightning Source LLC
LaVergne TN
LVHW021746060526
838200LV00052B/3498